BACKLASH
PRESS

A pioneering publishing house dedicated to creating intelligent, vivid books.

Established to inform, educate, entertain and provoke.

A Backlash Book
First published 2015
Reprinted 2024

backlashpress.com
ISBN: 978-1-0686972-2-7

Designer:
The Scrutineer, Rachael Adams.
Fonts: Baskerville, Bree serif.
Printed and bound by IngramSpark.

All rights reserved. No part of this publication may be reproduced, stored in a retrieval system or transmitted in any form or by any means, electronic, mechanical, photocopying, recording or otherwise, without permission of the copyright holder.

Copyright © Gretchen Heffernan 2015
The moral rights of the contributors have been asserted.

Editor: Gret Heffernan

A poetry collection to be read as a continuous story inside a communal narrative.

Journal Two

Gretchen Heffernan

Karen Tilley's Sun Print I

What to do With a Corrosive Nature

You begin by mixing arsenic with sunlight.
On paper place a representation of yourself as idea, as inkling
and wait for the sun to bleed your image into sight.

The result is a shadow of blue,
the greater the poison, the deeper the hue,
sometimes, so much, the shadow can burn straight through.

And, yes, the burns have much to do with timing. C'est la vie.
But. Imagine your skin ironed flat like old onion paper
that porous, at moments, tenuous, parchment thin to transparency.

And all that you touch and what touches you, is an image let in
your mind, a mirror smeared with years of markings, soiled, and words
you use to filter through your imprints can be a lethal poison.

Or just enough poison to keep you haemorrhaging in the sun, so honest.
A shadow that burns itself without singeing, is beautiful, is solaced.

Contents

Ezekiel Black	The Uncertain Trumpet	11
Keegan Lester	finding ways: para america	14
Ezekiel Black	Ham	18
Walter Dain	Easy Rain	20
Erica Bernheim	Trophy	22
Clifford Parody	Suburbia: A Litany	23
Julia Rose Lewis	Object of Reality: A Love Poem	25
Keegan Lester	at the time	27
Walter Dain	Photo	29
Keegan Lester	[ ]	30
R.G. Evans	In That Game Where We Make Our Porn Star Names	32
Mark Young	In bed with the Rosicrucians	34
Walter Dain	Memorial Window	35
Beth Somerford	Of Night Skies	37
Keegan Lester	Dating in New York	38
Mather Schneider	Poet's Bios	41
R.G. Evans	Wallace Stevens Speaks To Me In Dreams (Because He Doesn't Speak To Me On The Page)	44
Clifford Parody	We Try To Keep	46
R.G. Evans	The One-Armed Gravedigger	48
Alex Brockhurst	Postcard from Paris	49
R.G. Evans	from Oscillating Echoes	50
Michael Lee Johnson	Jesus in the Snow	52
Ezekiel Black	A Classic	53
Mark Young	Lifestyles of the Rich & Famous	55

Walter Dain	The Grocer	57
Michael Lee Johnson	The Drifter	58
Clifford Parody	Elegy for my father who is still alive	59
Walter Dain	Graduation Day	61
Anne Babson	River Canto	62
Sidney Ledlie	So Final	63
Keegan Lester	to my twenties	65
Anne Babson	What The Executioner Could Not Know	68
Michael Lee Johnson	Lily, Lonely Trailer Prostitute	71
Jessie Carty	Shopping After the Apocalypse (1)	72
Alex Brockhurst	Confession	74
Beth Somerford	Bed	75
Anne Babson	The Letter Thorn	76
Mark Young	A line from Harpo Marx	77
Beth Somerford	Minding The Kids	78
Julia Rose Lewis	Do I shove the man or the wall between?	79
R.G. Evans	When Religions Are Interested In Me	80
Anne Babson	But Thanks Be To God	81
Mather Schneider	Poetry Book Reviews	83
Julia Rose Lewis	Untitled	86
Joe Milford	Aesthete	87

Ezekiel Black

The Uncertain Trumpet

O

sacrifice
the

broken
bed

O offer
the question
that

lays [sic]
in

the grain
there, rot is

the

burden
borne by
an ax

O
to save

even the
down

is
sin
I

bestride ash like a co-
lossus.

I

a_m

omnibus

This
perverse
b
e
d

did
muddle

the Old Order
I

blow the trumpet
;

Keegan Lester

finding ways: para america

and that morning
is night now too.

the next morning from bed where you told me
i was walking ovals
looking at the desk
and flower and refrigerator.

the telling me part

is what scares me.
had all the people pointing

and lifted by it,

and hooing and hauing

with the lights turned down
from the corner of the auditorium

because you wouldn't do
what they would.

i was the road in Idaho

i was driven off of. i was the ditch i was

driven into, too. i became the people
who said i couldn't

love you like this until i stopped being
that way. and we a pocket of stars,

feet on the dashboard
etc, etc. etc. hush. we the moonlight

marking them for dead. the moonlight: the black spot
on the page of the bible
you tore just for me.

the moonlight: the black spot flowering

our matching bruises the size of my thumb
over our lungs, that we can't see yet.

that we infer from the bottom of the ashtray
in the windowsill.
you said *i'm going to kill you fucking dead*
and i smiled

because i love you.

and you say *it's because of the way your suspenders hang on the chair when you're gone...*

i think you mean it this time.
you imagined
a night stitched with night

like a baseball and tadpoles
and bazzoka gum, but did you have to
 tell me about it? laying us to rest

like this: our bodies beneath a sheet
of ice. our bodies caught
in the talons of two birds

above the city in which i love you, above what is caught

in power line wire

and our bodies aging
into taunt latex balloons
that haven't floated for them in years.

fawning, our bodies the dusty snout

of what we abandon
to see what it's life turns into
years later with a hidden camera

from a far.

and we make great television

to make great art
to make great television
we never wanted

for the people that never wanted us
to be in their lives in the first place.

Ezekiel Black

ham

if

a neighbour

is a
battle

The noun

ham

is like an airstrike
, and the
Commitment

drones

foreign

in the

committed

The

ex-
change

had
been frank
, if somewhat general.
The next meeting
will

involve

a tense dinner

during which the
guest

s_a_y_s

"I found the North Koreans

Walter Dain

Easy Rain

Round here they swear to go straight, not for the sake
of swearing but to lay low – rumour, best barometer.
Padres, imams, down-on-their-luck salesmen, mister
fix its, happy clappers, men with clipboards, rake
past houses with 'X's on doors in low weather.
A woman in stranger's garb sniffs rain. She chases urchins,
transfixed by the length of streets and the height of fences
and the wheel of birds over the roofs of houses. A man
in a trance mind maps a wall as day eeks out his question.
Contemptuous, a widow in weeds holds up beads to the Virgin.
Talk lasts the length of a shadow. Talk singes the smile of habit.
She fights back silence – talk, an assassin on bad soundtrack.
Strays skirt edges, trees fidget, the river's nervous. An old man sits
in a corner, looks for sense in days still left him, dares not look back.

Shapes contort where a horseman in stone
raises a charge against grass but stands alone.
A low slung car throttles and phases.
In a black-rimmed hat a tender aged lass
slouches her back to a pillar. She packs a knife
to ape the boss and the boss calls strangers lice.
Incognito, new glass towers grab the night.

Rain sweeps the wind's waltz in street light.
Under a slow dropping storm crow-men
criss-cross headlights from bin to bin.
Sixth floor, clean fingers click shut a bracelet.
She approves her mirror image but fidgets.
Her head's asunder. Her sensational book upsets.
Life's not like that. She turns a page, edges to rest.

Friday p.m., meat spits on a hob. Across the floor
voices sink behind him. He smooth's his thin hair.
A song on wire kicks the blues through cooked air.
His woman's heist of freedom sours in her mirror.
His fists, his fists beat his chest; he laughs, devil may care.
Ground pepper. He stands his dignity on a few small vices.
At table men hog newspapers to shut out the masses.
Waiters slink past women who snitch glances from faces.
Black dog's yawn. Lips in septic patter purse so like kisses.
A thinking man in a skull cap grooms his grey moustache.
Someone's fingers drum. Stares salt the huckster, flesh.
One man's newspaper: 'Troops mass on border'.
Step up, step up. Boots dust up the sky: the old slaughter.

Erica Bernheim

Trophy

The only thing moving in this airport is the train.
We appear enormous and geo-thermic.
The doors open the doors close.
The shrimp senses danger, but it's too late.
Cannibalism is camouflage.
To feel no fear is to have no brain.
Sticky and toxic, your filaments will live
in this fetal world of clauses and by-laws.

Clifford Parody

Suburbia: A Litany

We reach
for ourselves and find one another
breathless, arms outstretched, coming together
we disintegrate, we are tense, straining, sweat seeping
through forehead pores not yet dripping
along the creek bed, breasts pressed to a screen door
eyes closed and this SUV is uncomfortable,
as is the one that follows, and the Chrysler in between,
the trucks that will come later,
the tiny Mercedes and the sweatpants stumbling
blindly into bedrooms and the bathrooms,
apartments, trailers, houses, jeans ripped
on tall fences and codes forgotten,
horizontal mirrors and too many people,
(there is never enough music, there is never enough people)
rooftops of houses and schools, a twelve foot teepee
on fire, the studio with no heat, we speak
like starvation, the beautiful drugs are gone,
skin warm fingering the holes in a pair of leggings, running
back home to drop-top Beatles and parking lot tears,
glass shattered kicked under tables
with blues and American beer, backrubs and blows jobs,
those who help but are not needed, pillows on the bonfire,
community service, panties stolen from Macy's,

child proof seals, a rolled up bill alongside a crystal container
of potpourri on the back of a toilet
in the bathroom of a Joann Fabrics, digging
deeper into packs and pockets, pawn shop patronage,
pocket knives and cans, nicotine stained ceilings,
running and waiting, the half and the whole
and two or three more, tired eyes like cigarettes burning
through thighs and his skin
is not supposed to be blue
someone slap him—
tightening belts, tightening teeth,
the hardwood floor is cold.
        We reach.

Julia Rose Lewis

Object of Reality: A Love Poem

("My fruitbat, my gewgaw. You had me at no duh." Dora Malech)

She is the horse of my life, la belle et la bete.
Apollo's lady turned into tiger lily, why a tiger and not a calla lily? because bitey.
My blooming mare, my eastie-beastie.

She is the proud owner of a German passport
with the dimensions of her vagina. The name plate from her stall
follows me around the world.

My washable velvet, my Mecklenburg
also little miss safety, she always lands underneath me.
Splinter spots and monster cybermen do not phase her.

She is the time and relative dimension in space. She is objective reality
in a blanket of that blue; I would use the sonic hoof pick. The blue
of the journal, her brand tattooed on me.

My bearded lady, my fairy horse,
her fair tea, she drinks it double strong, double sweet, without cow's milk, of course!
She rejects veganism and vegetarianism in favor of hotdogs.

She does not perspire well; we hate it come summer.
Winter then, is her season for florida oranges, neither tangerines, nor clementines.
My fruit-loop lover, my psycho-bitch,
she is the builder upper of the greatest of poop castles.

Keegan Lester

at the time

i like it when you grab me
by the neck and bite me to prove facts.
i feel i have something worth recollecting
later on like world war one,
when you could pick any country you wanted
to fight for, and just fight for it, learning to
hate a stranger's foreign words
enough to think them similar
to a peach, both beautiful and hairy
and a sunset leading to a stomach
full of bayonet making that stomach
bloom and burst and cringe
an orchid in its own field
then go into town at night for whiskey and cinema,
maybe a blowie in an alleyway
depending on which country you chose to fight for. i was drunk
when someone tried to explain diplomacy to me:
if country a wants country b, then country a calculates
the resource expenditures it would take
to gain country b, verses the total sum of resources gained.
no one at this wedding thought
let's just leave country b alone, lets just stick
to hunting people for sport and the hustle
except me, but i was twelve and algebra confusing.

but maybe that was a lie. i can remember telling someone in the nineties
joining the marines is a good idea.
i didn't know there were still wars left to be fought
and where else to begin but with foxes:
foxholes just make war seem sexier
even though the evidence leans toward
a planet that's lost its axis.

Walter Dain

Photo

Eyes brim in a surprised face,
hair tossed, fingers fret.
On sepia lips a word starts.
Out a bay window,
a big oak flirts in green
with coquettish breezes.
On her lap sheet music.
The protest, plea, unsaid,
rings in a vase, empty
on a window sill.
Bunch of flowers
left to wait on a table.

Money's good, art delinquent,
Ach! 'Who can paint scent?'

Keegan Lester

[   ]

that usually what we claim stakes to was someone else's before us.
the lanterns in the night that meant safety, culturally repurposed into moons
and stars and the uterus in the backyards where smokers congregate.
at what age were we supposed to learn some humans are worth more
than other humans. at what age are children supposed to learn that.
the train kept training through the countryside without me and
growing up lonely,
i did not need to know to resist it. who are these people that enter us,
momentarily. on the television i watched cops beat a child until he was
nothing.
on the television i watched cops shoot a child until the air in his lungs
once used
to say *i love you mother* pooled in blood until the pressure from that
weight grew
heavy and became a stone and air was no longer enough to push that
stone,
to make those lungs move. on the news i watched an old man tell a
woman
she could not get pregnant from a legitimate rape, meaning she could
i assume: sweat the semen out, perhaps on the way home from the
assailants house
or her house, or her mother's house or the university that should have
protected her...

on the television i don't see women of color, or queer women of color or
the non-white male queer at all on the news, but, I am almost sure that cops
are beating them until they are no longer people and shooting them too,
until they can no longer say *I love you mother.* to be invisible is not the same
as to not exist. both invisibility and existence become the choice
of the observer, and for that i ask that we stop killing the children of america.
i ask that we stop making them invisible as well. i ask that we go to our sisters,
our mothers and grandmothers, that we repurpose the moonlight for them—
in their words, not ours.

R.G. Evans

In That Game Where We Make Our Porn Star Names

First name, name of your first pet.
Last name, name of the street where you grew up.

That's how it's done in Chick-A-Wow-Wow Land.
My resume is classified,

but you should know I have every qualification.
I am good at what I do, though what I do

is as secret as my passport
and its purple ink that you will never see.

Belfast. Belgian Congo. Bosnia.
And those are only the Bs.

Now I'm semi-retired: no more
late-night calls, helipads,

armored cars with tinted windows.
More time for lights, camera, action.

More face time with Trinka Morningside.
More time for cigs, after, with Ginger Red Toad.

More time for sharing with Pussywillow Vine
and Thor Shadowbrook. But sometimes

after the money shot (sometimes during,
but I'll never tell) my attention span is scrambled

and I imagine I smell jungle rot. Cordite
in the Afghani heat. Defoliant. Debriefing rooms.

Delight.
And if my phone should ever ring and I'm at work

(Flying Dutchman, Twisted Sister),
they wouldn't have to ask me twice.

To strive, to seek, to find, and not to yield,
as the poet said. I would drop everything

(forgive me, Pussywillow) and proudly say,
Colonel Decker, reporting for duty.

Mark Young

In bed with the Rosicrucians

She boarded a higher
plane, in the middle
of which was a kettle of
polished copper. Louis
T. Culling, in his *Manual
of Sex Magich*, referred to

that triangular sepulcher
as a vagina, & went on
to name it "cucurbit"—
a curious choice given
the inherently phallic
nature of the cucumber.

Walter Dain

Memorial Window

Butcher's son, he smiles past guests to his seat,
shakes many a hand; his pride, a black armband:
third son of a third son of a man
who boasted, with carver readied
for the joint, of easy meat.
Slice by slice oozes pleasure
gratis on a platter. With a broad swagger,
this man could tell how long a bird had to hang,
drip dry, before oven and tongue.

Two solid chaps position a chaise longue
beneath the tall window where soldiers
mangle together in a glass concoction.
Old dogs jaw-jaw old wars – attack, attack -
and in a lobby deploy again, mistakes redacted,
canon on the flank; padre's excuse-me yawn.
A small child pads down a corridor. Small cry.
Whisperers. Raised eyebrows. Who? Why?

All night beyond the bay window, a mad ocean,
trade botched. Oven fired, like a man in sin
the baker wrings his hands in his apron,
prays for a break in the weather. He counts
the cost on his fingers. This week, Remembrance.

Not a brother fell but on strangers' lands.

Dusk sickened as a town's sons had filed past a window
where a chase of limbs tangled the shadows.
Home bred lads, unused to slow kisses,
their chests swelled to the cant of home airs.
In step to the suck of sea on the harbour walls
they dreamed on, paid no heed to the hoarse choir
of fishermen, in the sink of day, sell all sorts and sizes:
lined up on the pier, the catch laid out in boxes.

Beth Somerford

Of Night Skies,

and how we peered in parallel,
out of the cracked pane, at
our pin-pricked mantel;
noticed that the sky is clearer
here, the stars insistent. How
we constellated our hands,
aligning the palms to match up
our flaws and sketch alive the
imaged figure - bones laughing
like shadows reversed - fizzing
in noise on the phosphor plate.

Keegan Lester

Dating in New York

i don't want to be
saved by my lover,
my lover says to me
with her eyes closed
on a park bench,
and the al pastor was
a little too chewy
and our stomachs turn
us into less sexy versions
of our selves in our heads,
but we are old now
anyways and sexy is relative.
we are like two
thirteen year olds
at a dance on opposite sides
of the room, waiting
to make a move
 and our eyes meet
during that country grammar song
and nelly's syntax
makes us believe
in what entire flocks of seagulls
can be capable of,
miles from a beach.

every time a person takes a selfie,
a piece of them dies
a little, a sacrifice
to the selfie gods, she says.
grow a beard and close your eyes
when you kiss me,
she says, with her eyes closed.
i don't want the fireworks
in the street to be
terrifying, but they are
and i know
i'd make a terrible soldier,
i say, every time i look
in the mirror and i know
i shouldn't be telling you all this
here but i don't
want to be saved by my lover either.
i want there to be pomegranates
and dark chocolate
and the kind of mountains
mouths make when at rest
at the kitchen table tomorrow morning.
in florida the mangroves hide
egrets and manatees and fish

and budweiser cans too
she says to me, as if
they are all the same thing.
and maybe she's right.
florida is the last place in this country
where it's still legal

if you're in a pinch, to bury
what you value
in a chest deep inside something else
for others to find later on
and in florida it's still legal
to have sex
on high school football fields
and smoke in bowling alleys,
she says. *and it's alright,
i mean, i'm not perfect either.*
there are entire bodies
of water that people call ocean,
and ocean is the name for both
the space we can not fathom seeing
and the surface
and i want to be
your gremlin fish
with a light above my head,
searching in the black
black water, i say.

Mather Schneider

Poets' Bios

"I am just
a teller of tales, eternally grateful for this
opportunity to amaze and entertain."

"I love to inhabit my imagination
with characters that are nothing like me
and yet, somehow
eerily familiar."

"My stories are like my children,
I nurture them, I feed them, and they teach me
so many wondrous things."

"I love language, I just
love language so, so
very much."

"After being an addict for 2 excruciating months,
I turned to writing
and it saved me.
I hope my writing might save others."

"Perfectly ordered words are my nirvana."

"My carefully crafted words can be found in...
(list of 94 journals)"

"I made a lot of money
and retired at age 53, so I
took up the art
of writing."

"I just love to imagine
characters and put them in
motion. You never know what they
are going to do!"

"Things are depressing
in this world. I prefer not to
think about that. I make my own worlds."

"I do not command the muse. The muse
commands me.
The muse speaks through me.
I am a conduit.
You can't question
the muse, you must simply allow it to
flow through you."

"I started reading when I was
6 months old, so I guess you could say
it all started there."

"I have had every job imaginable, waitress to poetry

teacher to poetry adjunct teacher to
full time mother."

"If I could not write, I would die. Period."

"I am what one might term 'congenitally creative.'
I can't help it. My imagination simply
soars like an eagle. It's a blessing, and, of course,
a curse."

"Writing is next to godliness. And I say that
in all humility."

"I just like to paint pictures with words.
My pencil is my brush,
as it were."

"I have two BA's, an MA, an MFA and am working on
my PHD in creative writing
with an emphasis
on poetry. I have been published
in my hometown newspaper,
twice."

"I am just a humble chronicler of the
silliness, vanity and occasional tenderness
and holiness of man, much like the writers
of the bible."

R.G. Evans

Wallace Stevens Speaks To Me In Dreams (Because He Doesn't Speak To Me On The Page)

He and I are not one. He and I and black night are not one,
but his voice awakens within me as I dream, says

concupiscence and the lack of a good concordance
are not excuse enough; says

Anecdote of the Lazy Reading, says
Anecdote of the Internet-addled Mind, says

sing beyond the genius,
beyond the rage for order, says

have a mind of winter and let yourself be
haunted by white nightgowns, says

Anecdote of Resistance, says
Anecdote of the One Who's Lost His Way, says

I placed a jar in Tennessee and all you did
was lift it to your lips and drink, says

you will awaken and not know which to prefer:

the whistling or just after, says

all there is is just after just after
the finale of seem--and I know what he says

is true enough for dreams
if not the mind who dreams them.

Clifford Parody

We try to keep

All those secrets we hide
in the creases behind our
knees, buried between shoulder blades,
stitched to our napes, crammed deep
into the shallow dimples carved
into lower backs and cheeks.
Ciphers etched into the enamel
of our wisdom teeth, removed.
Hours spent sitting on the
bench in front of the auto-
matic door at Goodwill,
opening and closing my eyes,
looking for love at first sight.
Hours spent in quieter places,
breathing deeply – focusing –
trying to separate the souls,
distinguish between the bits of skin
suspended within – a connection.

My father told me to treat
women like gold, so I spent
years melting them down, trying
to form them into something
that would fit my wrists like

Houdini's handcuffs, knowing
escape was inevitable. "For
now," she said, "can we just look
forward to looking back on all this
laughing?" In a past life we broke
the same bones. In a past life only
one of us was able to mend. The
house we shared became the
basement in the house of night.
We lay in bed like lightning bolts.
We lie in bed like lockjaw.
The poem begins with the first
three letters of the alphabet, a
brown bag full of malted courage,
a fire too close to the house.

R.G. Evans

The One-Armed Gravedigger

never blames his tools

never leans on his shovel, waiting

understands the importance of time, yours and his

knows good work can't be rushed

always gets to work early, sometimes before anyone has even died

cuts the edges of earth straight from right to left

waits twice as long as he needs to after the last mourner has gone

shovels the earth back in reverently before tamping it down

feels self-conscious praying, but always says a prayer, after

can bend an elbow with the best when he knows he won't be needed

can count the times he wasn't needed on the fingers of one hand

Alex Brockhurst

Postcard from Paris

Yesterday (Tuesday)
we went to the market & saw
lots of meat cakes & clothes

I miss Jethro very much
but there is a school dog
& it is very friendly

We have beaten
another school three times
9-4, 3-0 & 1-0

The woods are massive
& went to the Louvre
saw Mona-Lisa & the victory statue

Please write soon
as some people here
have had a letter.

R.G. Evans

from Oscillating Echoes

26

each miracle
was a superstition of
generational syllables,

old clothing, stained, beyond
wearable comfort,

from language stems multilingual meanings
etching a truth into faith
that each reflection of
permissible bridges

carries spun patterns
into the listening trends
the fleeceable examine with closed,

inauspicious eyes

27

exterior phrases

found experiential dances
of wind and serenades of an hour's
devoted brilliance to appearing warm
near what touches whole in the fraction
of human intuition,
calligraphy's beautiful notation, ballad
echoes wearing sound in the reflectional
wandering of outward music, impersonation
of what interior decisions decorate with
modal hands, mutated heirlooms

28

what leaps
in the balance of a silent
recreation: *memory*
misstates and analyzes
angles of prior inexistence, leading
language

through illness and
obstacles benign to
the variances of themed
misinformation

Michael Lee Johnson

Jesus in the Snow

I find your footprints here in snow, fresh and broken.
Will your lawyer fragment me, talk to Jesus private tonight.
Will belief set me out of chains, battery acid, free?
Life here is a urinal.
Search moon-eye in lonely sea feel swim of exile, sandpaper spots on skin, do not torture me.
Even devil in hell has his standard, private harvest, his jukebox baby.
Jesus suffers with the poor feels lonely in distant planets shares visions of the moon.
Let me drive you home truck tracks, then you left footprints in snow.
Do you hear sounds on the radio, jukebox baby?
I copy over, print remains, over footprints in snow.

Ezekiel Black

A Classic

Here's a
story—
a
story
, to be exact,

, of course,
for
teenagers

tha_t

updates, namely

,
after all, the Shakespearean
tragedy of love undone by
th_e reds

recalling
an Honest

picture of

1950s garb

—right
down to the
brass buttons.

Mark Young

Lifestyles of the Rich & Famous

Because he had experienced neither, President Bush confused the words poetry & poverty.

He said:
Many in our country do not know the pain of poetry, but we can listen to those who do.

He said:
There is no poverty in the war in Iraq.

He said:
As all of us saw on television, there is some deep, persistent poetry in this region as well.

He said:
When I see poverty I run a mile.

He said:
We have a duty to confront this poetry with bold action.

He said:
Poverty? (grins) You'll have to talk to my wife about that.

He said:

It is the aim of this Administration to do away with poetry.

Walter Dain

The Grocer

A no-nonsense type, he scraped by
on as few principles as possible.
They were: no one votes for poverty,
other people are hell.

He papered over a messy affair
Of his twenties and a brief lull
on valium to cover the cracks.
Most of all he liked

old movies with a message. He used to smirk:
'Show me the poet who made a million'.
He still managed to die in his bed,
his principles intact.

Michael Lee Johnson

The Drifter

The drifter in the room is a stranger,
he is crazy, is Bigfoot with deer moccasins on—
monster of condominium rooms and dreams.
The drifter in this room used to be my friend.
He spoke straight sentences, they did not sound like poetry—
reverberated like a narrative, special lines good a few bad,
or stories being unwound by the tongue of a gentleman,
lip service, juggler of simple words to children.
The night is a dark believer in drifters,
they sound sober, affairs with the wind,
the 3 A.M. honking of the Metro trains.
Everything sleeps with a love, a nightmare at night.
The drifter.

Clifford Parody

Elegy for my father who is still alive

And one day, Dad,
you too will duck down the alleyway,
bare feet licking puddles pooled along the bricks,
a broken leg, a pocket full of silver dollars, it's not winter,
it's you and me and I will watch the dirty trail
of your gown, no, you're naked, yes, you are back in your prime,
hair longer like mine, a curl-cropped face, curls caressing
the nape of your neck as you walk amid dumpsters,
as you walk knowing what
you're doing not knowing where
you're going not knowing what you do
and to who. I will always watch you; I will
let the sun spring off steel, sear my unshielded eyes,
I will not blink, I will breathe you in while I can, I will whisper
"Oh breath of God breathe on me" even though I don't believe. It's
warm
and I will watch you; water dripping off the power lines,
water dripping down your muscled back, don't turn
around, don't turn, there will be no music only
ceaseless traffic, a series of magic tricks,
a series of tubes removed, I'm watching please
don't turn I would collapse. It is your turn to collapse,
it is okay if you collapse, even red woods collapse, and I'll
be patient, I will watch you; your calloused hand gripping a

Marlboro,
you will turn around and I won't fall. You will be young, your face not
the face under the head we shaved, your body not the body
that made those noises when it climbed the stairs, legs
powerful unbound by walkers and wheelchairs,
your shoulders broad, my shoulders,
my feet forward licking puddles pooled
along the bricks. I will wrap you in a sheet—
if you must go, let me carry you.

Walter Dain

Graduation Day

On his face the same spooks -
 remember his first day at college -
that shiny freshman look.

Underarm the Order of Ceremony's book,
 a corner folded on his one page.
On his face the same spooks.

A raised eyebrow, she took
 a nibble from a dish, showed her age
betrayed by that shiny freshman look.

She tried not to see his eyes seek
 escape from the maternal cage
or read on his face the same spooks.

His rite of passage, so to speak.
 A new myth maker owned the stage
despite that shiny freshman look.

A band broke into music,
 brassy, from a bygone age.
Still his face wore the same spooks
 and that shiny freshman look.

Anne Babson

River Canto

I wish I could promise you that I were not wrong;
The icebergs melt in this river's global warming.
The humidity cooks the world. It won't be long.

The lido deck's *chanteuse, décolletée,* sings her song.
She is tone deaf, if svelte, her lyrics alarming.
I wish I could promise you that I were not wrong.

This *bâteau mouche*'s cantos are Piaf's *fête's flons flons.*
The sea level rises? Begin plankton farming!
The humidity cooks the world. It won't be long.

The barman pours cocktails with water from a bong.
The hammock swing of waves is fatally charming.
I wish I could tell you that I were not wrong.

I extricate my thoughts with a pair of ice tongs.
They are slippery, melting, shrinking, unforming.
The humidity cooks the world. It won't be long.

How can the feeble age preach sermons to the strong?
My daughter, it is yourself you should be arming.
I wish I could tell you that I were not wrong.
The humidity cooks the world. It won't be long.

Sidney Ledlie

So Final

The last clods shroud the wound in the earth
hiding her as if she had never existed.
Silent human pillars stand with bowed heads
while anguished cries show their pain.

Do they mourn for that translucent corpse
Or do they fear their own dying?

We are a stones throw from death,
yet we linger,
not knowing,
how or when.

Almond blossoms sprinkle white confetti into the wind
and flowers pay their silent tribute
knowing they too will wither and die,
their fragrance but a dull memory.

Soon dry leaves will sweep the grave
shuffling their own epitaph:
"This death, so final."

All around a testimony to oblivion
written in concrete silence:

"This death, so final."

Keegan Lester

to my twenties

Write me common
as apple trees in Vermont
as piano keys in Vietnam
as something to be left,
as something to be held
as my mother humming the Beatles
in red streaked morning.
Write me as anything not dreaming,
because there is no place
to dream red-eyed.
Write me nights when the photographs
whispered in our bedroom
to each other about winter
in 1965, about finding another trilobite
by the river. How smooth even rocks
become in time.
Write me as a photograph
because it won't dream of the face
in the moon or its color, or at all.
It's something you can put your finger on,
that won't ever change.
Write me as an organ hook
to a gospel song
with handclaps and feet stomps.

Write me as my first styrofoam margarita
in McCarren park, as the orange
living room with a broken couch
i slept on before leaving each time
and the time i came back.
Write me as an apology
and then cross that out
because we don't do that here.
Write me as something needing
a home, and name that home:
everything, as if handfuls of paint
that melts into the river's mirror:

~

the maples' sap;
        the twigs on the banks

scratching water at the boat's edge;
        the wake's twitching;

a blue jay's song.
        all of it.

~

Write me as the vinyl
that sang to me
as the trees that sang to me
as the cars and lights of the city

that sang too.
Write me as each seismic ripple
with it's own a song.
The ocean, the pavement, the witching
hours, a lonely boy in a tree,
Write me as the color yellow:
a caged canary
in a coal mine,
someone else's poverty
that sang to me.
As the girl
waiting on a hunger
that sang to me too:

> *your mouth on me,*

> *be something in the wind*

> *like citrus,*

> *like something with fangs*

> *something broken*
> *and bleeding through*
> *its sutures.*

Anne Babson

What The Executioner Could Not Know

What the executioner could not know
as he pounded me into the powder
what the cutthroat could not know
as he trampled me with his heavy hooves

What the molester could not know
as he cracked my sections like a peeled orange
what the witch doctor could not know
as he pricked my doll body with the spikes

Was how right after the blood seeped deep
in the bloody mud, drowning the termites lurking
Was how right after the shivering had ceased
and the wind whisked the echoes to the poles

Was how right after the crowd diasporaed
and the scene was no more unseemly seen
Was how right after the silence mushroomed
and billowed out in concentric quiet ripples

That you would descend in a clock radio alarm blaring
of Hungarian rhapsody violins and hand-plucked mandolins
That you would descend in the clatter of a brass band
tumbling down the staircase of the Empire State Building

That you would descend in a cascading King Kong giggle --
the guffaws of all the first graders at the three-ring circus
That you would descend in samba, salsa, meringue, cha-cha --
a tribe of Tito Puentes shaking their maracas in unison

That you would unfurl the folds of your burlap robes
and envelop me in the heat of your mystical body in communion
That you would whip the licorice satin of your flying cape
around my shoulders and under my waiting armpits

That you would spread out the heliotrope velveteen of your smoking jacket
and wrap me in your first-draft manuscript of *Lady Windermere's Fan*
That you would extend wide the span inherited from the pterodactyls
and nestle me between the feathers of your copious white wing

That you would cradle my head, kiss my eyelashes, tenderly take me
aloft, aloft, aloft to your titillating, noisy, neon, erupting spice garden
That you would flurry me past the line and the velvet rope at the heavy doorway
onto the cushions of the cozy couch of the VIP lounge next to
who's who, who's really who.

Michael Lee Johnson

Lilly, Lonely Trailer Prostitute

Paint your face with cosmetic smiles.
Toss your breast around with synthetic plastic.
Don't leak single secrets to strangers-
locked in your trailer 8 foot wide by 50 foot long
with twisted carrots, cucumbers, weak batteries,
and colorful dildos-you've even give them names:
Adams's pleasure skin, big Ben on the raise, Rasputin:
the Mad Monk-oh no, no, no.
Your legs hang with the signed signatures
of playboys and drifters ink.
The lot rent went up again this year.
Paint your face with cosmetic smiles.

Jessie Carty

Shopping After the Apocalypse (1)

You start in your house. You weigh the pros and cons of each piece of luggage, each bag stored in the top of your closet. You set aside a black backpack you used to carry when teaching college courses and a messenger bag you bought in Kyoto which you discovered years later had a Made in China tag.

You pick out your favorite outfit. And then your second most favorite outfit. You pack the second. You think of Douglas Adams and select a nice sized towel. Coats are bulky so you choose a sweater.

You roll a thin blanket inside a yoga mat and use the combination of an overpriced yoga strap and velcro to attach the bedroll to the bottom of the backpack.

From your bathroom you compile a smaller bag with a toothbrush, band-aids, nail clippers, Neosporin, a collection of Aspirins and Ibuprofens. A comb. A brush. Find an unopened bar of donkey milk soap.

From the kitchen you set aside a can opener. A spoon. A fork. Your smallest pot. A cup. Add a bar towel.

You consider the knives. Decide to take the small switchblade from the junk drawer.

There are two side pockets on the backpack. You put water bottles in both.

In the laundry room you select a multi-tool. A flashlight. A handful of batteries.

You decide on only one USB cord and charger.

There is a special pouch in the backpack for pens so you fill it with your favorites and a few pencils. You allow yourself one notebook.

You wander from room to room, staring at the bookcases. You tell yourself that just having one book will be temporary. You close your eyes. Spin. Reach towards the shelf. You don't open your eyes until your backpack is zipped shut.

Alex Brockhurst

Confession

I have used the very last
of your matches

You explain over breakfast
they easily break
the striking strip inadequate
the box too loose a fit
spilling its cargo
on the unwary

This morning
rising early
I made my first cup
without putting my eyes in
not seeing the arrows
you had carefully penned
each end of the box

this way up
this way up
strike gently
away from the body
do not place spent matches
in the box

Beth Somerford

Bed
After *Divan Bed* by Mona Hatoum

It is as if she sleeps on a girder;
fearful of falling, of moving, lest
she give her awakeness away.
Hemmed in by scaffolding, she
has poured herself onto the bed;
posted her limbs in position.
She lies a thousand feet above
the bedroom carpet; her thighs
motted by steel, arms adorned
with thumbprint bracelets.
Most nights there is a muddling
of limbs, a voiceless barter,
like the scrabble of flyovers.
Her ribs are iron struts, her hips
a hiding place. She has turned
herself inside out. She knows
if he knew, he would crack her
like a fortune cookie.

Anne Babson

The Letter Thorn

On *The Lyndsfarne Gospels*, stuck like a tethered thorn
Through the Old English parchment, preens the letter thorn.

Her pains multiplied. They bloated fecund. She felt guilt
Triplet, quintuplet sorrow, octuplet her thorn.

After momma's burial – the casino! They
Gambled her grave flowers, even bet her thorn.

Today, if a man wants to win big, he fights for
First blood, breaking rivals' skin with his go-getter thorn.

The sportsman snags in the swamp with a brambled pole,
Snaring mud fish and stone fish with his netter thorn.

He was competitive about everything!
On his crucifix head, he claimed a better thorn.

It doesn't make sense any more to garden, she thought,
If watering a rose requires a wetter thorn.

Old English, meet this new American woman.
Runes from her berry bushes, Anne has met her thorn.

Mark Young

A line from Harpo Marx

Something unexpected is
happening, an attitudinal shift
away from broken families
tricking out run-down

Manhattan walk-ups. *La
vecchia cultura cade*. Out of love
with the political religion
of the nation. Instead an

incredible five & a half hour
mixtape of old Scottish songs
that see hormonal issues as weak
or a barrier to a successful career.

Total Apostasy. The old tenement
no longer being rebuilt, no longer
using Old Maiden Aunt hand-
painted yarn. Drunks vomit cars.

Beth Somerford

Minding The Kids

I guess what he meant about the ice cream
when his cell phone... when his *wife*
rang, was that he was treating the kids

to something special and that the beer
was somehow incidental. They are togged
up for the beach with toweling backpacks –

deckchair stripes - and fearful quiet as
they play by the lake (he says 'they've
played by the lake'). For reasons

unexplained he's hard on them. He barks
constraints, 'stay here', 'sit down'
and threatens to go home. Then, oddly,

he reminds them, within earshot, within
eavesdrop, of the photos in his wallet,
their devotion. His words are sudden

saccharine. And from the terrace
of the bar, we sit and watch the heavy
weather come in off the lake.

Julia Rose Lewis

Do I shove the man or the wall between?

Three salted butters,
two plates so you do not butter your book.
Murmur wrung;

it was an old tree.
It remembers trail blazing the wealds.
What is the difference between a wall made of wood and a fence?

The silent love in would.

R.G. Evans

When Religions Are Interested In Me

The time of year when my father's blood rises
through the arbor, the vine's fiddlehead feelers
blowing up bunches of grapes like balloons,
when I wait for fruit to ripen, the sugary smell
of days I would have saved like fireflies in a jar.
The time of year when every woman's hips look like
they'd fit me like a grave, when men my age speak
of grandchildren and their love sounds like a lie,
impossible as the fact that I am growing young
inside this graying skin, impossible as all these dreams
that cling to me like lichen. The time of year when
yesterday's music seems yet unwritten.
The time of year when books whisper to me
from their shelves but grow mute the moment I look inside.
The time when power hums in wires over my head
and my mother, three states distant and six feet deep,
hums me a lullaby she never sang. The time of year
when the year knows its time is almost up,
when its months have names that end in *ember*.
The time of year when the weary try to start again
and the rest listen too closely to the great machine,
where I think my father's blood is used for oil,
that time of year when I awake to dreams.

Anne Babson

But Thanks Be To God

"But thanks be to God, which giveth us the victory through our Lord Jesus Christ." – 1 Corinthians 15:57

"And I will give unto thee, and to thy seed after thee, the land wherein thou art a stranger, all the land of Canaan, for an everlasting possession; and I will be their God." – Genesis 17:8

But thanks be to God -- one of us had to go
First, someone had to trek through the underbrush,
    Bearing and brandishing a two-edged
    Machete to cut serpentine ferns out

Of the Okeefenokee swamp opening
The path to something much wilder than any
    Ponce-de-Leon-dreamed-of fountain of
    Youth, merely youth renewed, much richer than

Candide's departed El Dorado pursued
Passionately by conquistador after
    Conquistador for cash, merely cash,
    Much more useful than the Northwest Passage,

Henry Hudson's ultimate commuter tool
Elusive as a fast lane entering the

Holland Tunnel, and this just for speed,
    Much more practical than the manifest

Destiny discovered by Jefferson's men
Like papooses on Sacajawea's back,
    For we are, despite our heaviness,
    Carried across all the Rockies by Him.

But thanks be to God, as we couldn't survive
The yellow fever of our own filth, all we
    Long-wandering Jamestowns waiting to
    Perish in the climate of this promised

Territory, were we to enter on our
Own. Someone had to offer Himself up
    Meat for this Donner Party band of
    Survivors. Someone had to say in this

Perilous place, "I am the only right way
To circumnavigate, darling explorers.
    Follow this map, only this single
    Cartography, to discover Vineland."

Mather Schneider

Poetry Book Reviews

The literary voices
the confident literary voices
with satiny literary tones
uttering profound
wise-behind-their-ears
words
such as

"Samsun Waldorf Wickenstick-Farley
exposes the current reality
by dismantling
the outworn patriarchal system
with startling use of
imagistic
juxtaposition"

or

"Bethany Polygot Narthoopial-Figenstein
commands a brilliant technique
and makes the courageous decision to
not make grammatical sense
which transports the reader to another
realm

of existence"

or

"Samoj Pannoven has seen it all
and renders his world in perfect-pitch, you miss
this 2nd year MFA student
from Carthington University
at your own peril"

or

"Moofus Pergleesius Nanomite-Smith III
confines his paragraphs to short single
sentences
and in so doing forces the
reader to confront the inevitability of his own
transient nature"

or

"Joel Wallet-Chain tells it like it is
and knocks you out of your comfort zone
like a shot of morphine in the
penis"

or

"Ocean Yin-Yan Wongfist
shoots his cum-wad of primordial soup

like an articulation of chewed-up stars"

Julia Rose Lewis

Untitled

The poet's answer:

Yes, Adam can cast a shadow. Shadows are good, beautiful. Truth and beauty and negative capability, Keats casts a shadow over us.

The chemist's answer:

In 2012, a group at the University of Brisbane was able to demonstrate the absorption imaging of a single atom of ytterbium by laser. "A single atom scattering resonant light can closely approach these limits, making it an excellent test system for investigating fundamental limits to imaging... In particular, the dynamics of chromatin in living cells [13] could be imaged without delivering a lethal UV dose." I have printed out a copy of the paper, if you would like to read it.

A third of an answer:

Both scientists and poets should be careful of gratuitous acts of anthropomorphisation and personification. It is something that I am playing with in my dissertation. I would like to see you. Maybe here?

Joe Milford

aesthete

was my proclivity to beauty too acute? or
was beauty just to be mine at all times? or
was the beautiful using me for its own arpeggio? or
was i just lucky at all turns in the labyrinth to hear
a gorgeous sultry sonorous ergo? or would i become beautiful if all i did
was pursue the beautiful? the most attractive "NO" imbues. or were
we all anthropologists of our own inner beauty? i always thought i was
something a scarecrow dropped that a superhero picked up and then
discarded once he became human again. beautiful mushroom. ugly
beautiful vomit of light snuffing itself on. gorgeous pungent. beauty,
you hold the dead butterfly in your hand and say it's not symbolic
while you smile a highway towards a short film festival of very beautiful
mavens among marvelous concepts. i think that, as a boy, i just realized
that i had to do everything possible, if i could, to stay a boy, as long as
i could, because, well, that was where all bras were slingshots, all ice
creams were the last and all ice creams were the first.

www.ingramcontent.com/pod-product-compliance
Lightning Source LLC
Chambersburg PA
CBHW030455010526
44118CB00011B/952